LOOK
Feel
BECOME

BRIAN ROSCOE

LOOK, FEEL, BECOME
COPYRIGHT © 2021 BY BRIAN ROSCOE

All rights reserved. No part of this publication may be reproduced, distributed, or transmitted in any form or by any means, including photocopying, recording, or other electronic or mechanical methods, without the prior written permission of the author, except in the case of brief quotations embodied in critical reviews and certain other noncommercial uses permitted by copyright law.

The content of this book is for general informational purposes only. It is not meant to be used, nor should it be used, to diagnose or treat any medical condition or to replace the services of your physician or other healthcare provider. The advice and strategies contained in the book may not be suitable for all readers.

Neither the author, publisher, nor any of their employees or representatives guarantees the accuracy of information in this book or its usefulness to a particular reader, nor are they responsible for any damage or negative consequence that may result from any treatment, action taken, or inaction by any person reading or following the information in this book.

For permission requests or to contact the author, visit:
brianroscoeauthor.com

ISBN-13: 978-1-957348-03-2

PRINTED IN THE UNITED STATES OF AMERICA

LOOK Feel BECOME

"People say that what we are all seeking is a meaning for life. I think that what we're really seeking is an experience of being alive, so that our life experiences on the purely physical plane will have residence within our innermost being and reality, so that we can actually feel the rapture of being alive."
-Joseph Campbell

Throughout this book, as you encounter particular entries and concepts, you may be asked to apply questions to certain entries using the exercise Look-Feel-Become. It's a powerful exercise that you can use to empower your personal transformation.

For example, let's take the personal goal of "living life with a deeper state of inner ease:"

APPLY LOOK: What does your "deeper state of ease" look like in your mind? Create an intellectual picture, a framework of sorts, that helps you cognitively define what the concept of inner ease means to you. What does it look like? This is a vision to build on, to construct basic understanding around your goal. Ask yourself questions like: What's the quality of my body function when I'm in this state of inner ease? What is the tone of my mind? Are things different? How do I breathe, sit, and hold my facial muscles? Do I hold them differently? Are my mind's ruminations, addictions, and diet choices the same when I'm at ease?

As your improved tone of the mind reflects in the body, how will you walk forward in your deeper state of inner ease? Will your personal habits, judgments, or capacity to love change in any way? Make a mental note of all these things that define what your goal looks like.

APPLY FEEL: When you're done with Look, ask yourself: How does it feel, deep within my heart, to be in a deeper state of ease? Here, we're going past the intellectual framework of the mind and delving into the soul of the change. In essence, its heart gift. What does it really feel like in the being of who you are to be in that deep state of "inner ease?" How does your body, mind, and spirit feel in that desirable state of being? Be present with that feeling—allow yourself to absorb into and be heart-centered with it. This is how we live through our heart.

APPLY BECOME: And, finally, who do you become? What essence of you comes forward when you embody your new way of thinking and feeling into your walking world? How do you interact in life? Who are you when you're present in a deeper state of inner ease as you relate to yourself and others? Does it change how you interact with those you love, or who you are in your life? Who do you become?

These questions can help us understand, move into, and more fully embrace our goals of personal growth and transformation. They allow us to successfully approach our internal and ancient desire of remembering our truth—desires of life that, one way or another, consciously or subconsciously, we're all striving towards. It helps us satisfy our very human goal of living in our heart. We open ourselves to becoming, once again, who we are meant to be.

LOOK
Feel
BECOME
JOURNAL

As you work through the different entries and lessons in this book, you're likely to find some areas that strongly resonate with you, and you'll probably come across ones that irritate you as well. Pay attention, these are the topics you might want to take notes on, it's these subjects and ideas that are showing you where some of your most valuable self-work is needed and located, and it's a great place to apply the concept of Look, Feel, Become. If you feel like it, jot down your perception and any points of wisdom that you take away from these studies, take notes on, mark and underline words and phrases, or simply fold over a page to mark the spot that touched your internal self. You'll more than likely want to come back to them again. It can be interesting to observe how subjects of the heart tend to evolve within us over time.

There's intentional open space on many of the pages in these books that have been set aside specifically to take notes on, so don't be shy. It's your book, your journey. Mark it up. Your inspired moments are too important not to record and remember. Having something you can come back to for review and clarification when needed can be helpful. It's like remembering the strength and meaning behind a Power Statement we love and live by, or tapping into a meaningful memory that we've drawn energy or wisdom from in the past. It's good to have a trigger to draw us back.

NOTE: Keep in mind that as you're exploring Look, Feel, Become, the changes you're trying to make and hold onto within yourself can usually be divided into two sections:

- First, what qualities of behavior or thought would you like to include in your life?

- Second, what qualities would you like to eliminate from your thinking and behavior?

Two directions, one goal: creating a heart-driven life experience on this journey.

LOOK
Feel
BECOME
softening my mind and heart

This is an example of how I've used Look, Feel, Become in my personal life. One of the qualities I've struggled with for years is a hardness to my interaction with myself and others. I don't know if it came from my genetic coding, a learned behavior from family, or personal heartbreak of some kind, but it rears its head frequently, especially with those I love most. I find myself getting rigid in my thinking and stubborn in my expectations of how life should be for me, my family, and my community. It's a hardness of heart that feels very limiting to my much larger goal of knowing love.

So, I see myself through the steps of
Look, Feel, Become:

What does it look like in my mind to interact with people and myself in a softer way, with more compassion and kindness?

What does that look like?

LOOKING: What does softer look like? When we look at an idea we want to embrace, we're establishing an intellectual conversation with it, trying to paint a picture in the mind so we can visualize a structure around what we're trying to create in our world.

For me, I want to understand what living my life in "a softer way" looks like. How would I describe the concept of "softer living" to myself or someone else if I wanted to build the idea in their mind? How would I paint a word picture in the mind of what it is to "live softer?"

So then, what would it be like, what might it look like, to walk through life in a softer way? Without so much judgment, without an attachment to your opinion about things, without getting rigid as soon as you hear about politics that don't agree with your position—what would it look like if you saw people with kindness, even those who haven't treated you well? What would it look like if you saw yourself in a gentle, loving way, no matter what you were struggling with in the moment?

FEEL SOFTER: This is more a question of the heart. How would it feel, for example, to live life in a softer way in the deepest part of who you are? How would that feel to your heart? How would that feed into your attitude and the way you walk in life? There aren't a lot of words to describe this, but you can hold on tight to the feeling that gets cultivated when you entertain the concept of being softer.

BECOME SOFTER: Who do you become when you are soft? We know what it looks like, we know how it feels, so who are we then when we walk softly and live without that hard, crusty layer influencing us? The answer is always the same when we are establishing qualities of the heart within: we become ourselves. We become ourselves because only the truth of who we are can come forward when we establish qualities within us that are fed by love.

Explore your heart!

Explore all the different qualities that you want to identify yourself through. What are you looking to become in this life? How do you want to walk forward and what qualities do you want to resonate towards the people you love? Start your list. Begin your exercise of looking, feeling, and becoming all of those beautiful things. Become yourself again!

EXPLORING THE BIG LOVE JOURNEY OF LOOK *Feel* BECOME

Ever find yourself feeling confused and wondering about the purpose of your journey in this world? Well here's a pretty good pointer: there's a huge part of life that's all about reclaiming your big love; recapturing the heart-love that is born through you. Some believe that knowing love is the only thing that's truly important in life. And this big love – this love that you already are – requires your attention to healthy self-care, it asks for compassion, and understanding for this world, as well as gratitude for your journey and the gifts presented. Our challenge to know love asks us to question the subtle influences of the subconscious and conscious mind around the struggles and difficulties we're engaging every day and to inquire about our personal motives in life.

Reclaiming our love asks us to explore the quality and tone of our thinking and begs us to stay open to a life of awakening and rejuvenation. This big love asks you to remember and explore your creativity. It requires you to participate in every possible attempt at knowing and loving yourself. Big love is about taking care of this world with honor, keeping the Earth and all its inhabitants safe and secure in their environment. It's about understanding those pesky seven deadly sins – pride, envy, gluttony, greed, lust, sloth, and wrath – the ones that regularly tempt us, and it's also about having their loving antidotes stored within our hearts, always at our disposal. Big love asks us to fully dedicate ourselves to our journey back toward heart, reclaim who we truly are, and to maintain a huge attention on staying awake and recognizing the amazing miracle of all that we are. Knowing big love is really what we're here for.

A short commentary on love.
The phrase; "the infinite forms of love," or "love in all its forms," will come up from time to time in my writing. And when you notice it, it's important to understand that love is not confined simply to the more familiar, socially comfortable forms, like romantic love, and the love of friends and family. Love is meant to be a part of everything we do, every event, situation, thought, action and interaction we have. Love can play

a role in whatever we participate in from child birth to how we wake up in the morning, from how we approach religion to our views of war, from our attitude at work to how we choose to spend our free time.

The struggles we experience due to our human nature do not restrict whether or not love can be present unless we consciously decide to choose its absence. It's my opinion that love needs to be a part of all of our best approaches, for everything we do. We need to give ourselves permission to be present to love in any situation we might encounter, because it's with an inner stance that understands the importance of love that we can live a life most true to ourselves.

Love can exist in all realms, we just need to allow it. We need to choose a life with strong healthy love, filled with integrity and understanding of what's most important to our human heart. A love that asks for strength from others and incorporates a stance of integrity is found the phrase "tough love" (a love requiring people to take responsibility for their actions, including ourselves). There's gentle love, healthy love, there's kind love, and compassionate love, there's strong love, and there's self love, there's a love with integrity, and love with a softness and understanding. The list can go on and on, because love is the defining energy behind everything we do and when we can bring it into our lives, we can remember more clearly who we are. If everything in this world can be approached with a healthy love, a love that refuses to do harm, an approach that refuses to leave people in pain, then we'll know that we've figured out love, and also figured out ourselves.

"Between stimulus and response, there is a space. In that space is our power to choose our response. In our response lies our growth and our freedom."
-Victor Frankl

YOU CAN EXPLORE ANYTHING WITH LOOK *Feel* BECOME

What do you want to experience in life? What feelings and emotions do you aspire to? And what wisdom do you want to embody? LFB is a self-evaluation and self-improvement tool that can help you create a framework around any desire to change. It can assist you in any goal you might have around your personal development. It's a simple technique that can be used in conjunction with any desire to develop your skills around a hobby, a personal interest, or work-related strength. But its most valuable application is in the area of heart-centered personal growth and expansion. It's an invaluable tool for waking up and refining your inner stance in life.

TAPPING INTO THE CREATIVITY OF WHO YOU ARE

Using the techniques of Look, Feel, Become (LFB), we can create powerful potentials of movement at the levels of body, mind, and spirit that have the capacity to help us shift and grow within ourselves. It helps us free up the stagnant energy of life that can be limiting to us, so that truth, our authentic nature, and the expression of love that we are can expand forward. Because unless you're moving through your pain, experiencing your human side, unless you're moving through life, unless you're learning and growing in the world, well… you're stagnating in it. **It's our job to step forward and produce movement for ourselves in whatever way we can.** No one can do it for us, but we have an uncanny ability to find our guides, tools, and best lessons that help point us in the directions that are wonderfully productive for our journey. That's what we're doing here, creating points of productivity. Productivity for living a more authentic and inspired life, a life based in exploring and uncovering our deepest truths. The techniques of Look, Feel, Become help us do that in their own unique way.

Our ultimate shift is always one of being and experiencing more love. All of us have such great capacity to become what we most desire. Often, our greatest challenge is to define exactly what that is. However, we have a gift deep within ourselves, it

lies beyond our ego, and the fear of not belonging, and it's past our feelings of not being enough, we all possess a core memory, a pure and authentic identity waiting for our attention. Deep down, we know it, we feel the presence of what we desire most already within us; we know that we are already what we so yearn to remember. It's the truth of our own love, a love held within us, though a love often forgotten. And this forgotten voices' only goal is to remind us of all that we're capable of, to remind us that we are indeed beings blessed with the spirit of all that unfolds from love's presence.

So yes, sometimes a little self-recalibration is called for in order to help us shift away from our old, inherited, unproductive patterning. Our goal is to move past the thinking and behaviors we've learned that simply no longer work, qualities that have no positive end. We need to get away from the thinking and behavior that causes us pain, fear, anxiety – ideas that keep us yearning for something different than this moment. We need to abandon the unproductive mindsets that only create a sense of disconnection from ourselves. And this is exactly where Look, Feel, Become (LFB) can be a valued tool of growth for us. It can help us explore and take control of who we're becoming on this precious journey.

Whether it's thoughts, beliefs, addictions, or behaviors, LFB can help us create and experience a healthy internal framework to rebuild ourselves with. It can act as a guide for internal direction as well as a clarifying tool that helps us understand the feelings, resistance, and human tendencies associated with life and change. LFB helps us point ourselves into the deep internal shifts we yearn for surrounding the challenges of being human in this world. It's a great tool of growth, worthy of your curiosity and your exploration.

LOOK
Feel
BECOME
a journey of change,
a process of life moving through us

In this section, we're first going to explore the art of opening up to areas of change. Our starting point will be to help you make a list for yourself – a list that expresses what you want to let go of and what you want to connect with on this human journey. And then we'll walk through the process of applying Look, Feel, Become to one of your topics, and I'll give you a personal example of how LFB can work. Pay attention to the example as it can help clarify how the technique might be used for your own personal journey and growth.

As you begin, keep in mind that any of our internal struggles are there to help us. They're the beacons that show us where we're stuck, where we need to grow, and they guide us on our path back to ourselves.

Let's face it, everyone has their glitches, their inconsistencies and imperfections, their addictions, and their weaknesses. And whether we're courageous enough to admit it or not, we all have a deep desire for growth and expansion beyond where we find ourselves in any given moment. We can't hide from our challenges and we can't ignore them. They exist as unlearned lessons and unrealized growth, and they want our attention. Our lessons, our growth, the challenges of this journey aren't just going to go away – not until we somehow find our way of healing them. So, no time like the present. If we can identify them, we can begin the journey of healing them.

Okay, Enough Said. Let's Begin.
Often, the biggest part of our journey is held in our quiet listening. Listening to the questions that our hearts pose as we experience ourselves in this world. It's a listening that requires us to live with curiosity, and to question our world using the words and feelings that best suit our hearts. It asks us to touch those answers that are held deep within. This is us, us on our journey, exploring and doing what we can in becoming our most natural best.

In applying LFB to the changes we want in our lives, we can get very specific. We can integrate it into any of our relationships, improving not only the relationship but our part in them. This might include cultivating healthier interactions with our life partners, our children, siblings and parents, interactions with friends, employers, co-workers and employees, even how we approach strangers. Or we can be very general about cultivating healing and new ways of being that have the potential to impact anyone. But we can retrofit LFB for anyone or anything that needs work. With Look Feel Become, we can impact whatever doesn't fit into the healthy, heart-centered mindset and inner stance that we desire for our life.

So go explore, look at what you want to change, who you want to become, and then pick your subject – something simple but meaningful to you. It might be an issue, a goal that you'd like to unblock yourself around, something you'd like to create healthier thinking, behavior, and internal change around. It's likely to be something you've thought about before. Some obvious trait that you want to change, or a personal goal you'd love to accomplish. So, look for the lessons that you know you need

– they're usually pretty in our faces already, we just need to identify them and jump in.

When we decide to explore a little deeper into this journey, it opens us up to thousands of new possibilities for our minds to entertain. The simple question, "What would I like to add to my journey, and what can I eliminate so that I can grow?" seems to have the power to swing the barn door wide open, and suddenly ALL the animals want out! So, have a pencil and paper handy at all times, because when you least expected it, the donkey wants out, and you didn't even know you had one! Take a note and, when the time is right, explore and grow.

Below are some basic topics that I commonly explore. It's just human stuff we all struggle with, but when we look a little deeper, sometimes we're surprised at the work that needs to be done. So, feel free to draw ideas from these examples as you explore:

SOFTNESS: Personally, I know that sometimes I can be harsher than I'd like with people. So I often explore how can I become softer in my world with the people I interact with, or even think about. I consider everyone – those who I work with, people around town and that I see at the store, the street panhandlers, and the people I'm close to and care deeply about. It's important to me to find ways to not cause pain for others. So, I often ask myself, "What would that look like?"

PATIENCE: Patience kind of resembles softness, but with maybe more of an internal twist to it. And impatience, well, that seems to be a core lesson for just about everyone. We all want and often need to figure out how to be more patient in life. It's a topic that can impact multiple areas of living. Whether it's finding an inner patience or our outward expression of impatience towards any of the workings of life, patience is a huge challenge for nearly all of us.

So, what does it look like to be more patient in life? What is it like to be less impatient with people in my world, or with the way things are going in my world? And what is it to be more patient with myself, with those I love, and with my community and larger family? What does it look like to simply embody more patience with my personal journey? Just overall, good old fashioned patience – it's huge. This is all so important and worth exploring and engaging in a big way.

NEGATIVITY: Negativity of any kind. We all have our moments of poisonous, toxic thinking, especially when we get stuck in difficulty and challenges. And we all express that negativity in our own unique, sometimes hidden, ways. So, take a good honest look at your most toxic and painful expressions of negativity and explore what the antidote might look like. What does it look like to take the charge down a notch, or more? Pay attention to who you become when you're stuck in negativity. And then imagine what it looks like to be free of it. Who are you in the absence of your negativity?

UNDERSTANDING:

In our understanding of one another we can also find our peace. And in that understanding, we tend to understand ourselves better, there's way more space for self-love. It's a win-win kind of game of the heart. A thought on understanding one another as ourselves was concisely and wonderfully written by the Roman playwright Terence. "I am human, so nothing human should be alien to me." In other words, we have the capacity to understand everything human, whether it's within us or someone else. Win-win! So then, what does it look like to open to myself and others with more tolerance, more understanding, and more compassion (they all seem to move as one)?

FREEDOM FROM JUDGMENT: As a good friend once said, "Nothing good ever comes from our judgment, either of ourselves or one another." But we all know we do it; we all participate in judgmental thinking! We just have to pay attention what happens to us when we're entangled in judgment and who we become when we're engaged in stepping away from it. In its most negative sense, when we're engaged in judgment, it seems to permeate every thought and colors the very quality of everything we interact with. There's simply no value in it. It's totally worth taking the time to explore learning how to set our judgment aside.

Yeah, I know! There's so much to work on! Where does all this stop?

Well, understanding what it is to be a person from the inside doesn't really ever stop. It's a journey that inevitably moves through you your whole life. Once you dive in, stopping is no longer an option. Our inner work defines a huge part of our journey, and embracing that deep inner yearn – the desire that we all have to know wisdom – and through that wisdom to find our seat in compassion makes everything we do to get there totally worth it. So, welcome to your journey. Yes, there's lots to do, but have heart, we are a resilient lot!

A short list for contemplation:

- Listening to the opinions of others without taking them personally.

- Sidestepping our stubborn adhesion to our own point of view. Not truly listening to others.

- Recognizing our addictions and our tendency to try and escape through them (compulsive thinking, food, drugs and alcohol, sex, consumerism, greed, excessive exercise, or anything else used to distract ourselves from being awake to our journey).

- Learning to be here, now, in a more present, mindful, New-Now way.

- Asking ourselves: What do we need to let go of or embrace so that we can move closer to our struggles and our goals with compassion for ourselves? So that we might explore being alive and human to them without getting stuck in them. Learn from a place of being in this heart-centered miracle, rather than stuck in our thinking minds.

LOOK Feel BECOME GRATITUDE

What do we want more than to know love? More than to live with gratitude and forgiveness? Is there anything that fulfills us more than living our truth? Or to be connected to and be in honor of our ultimate good? Can anything bring us the same "stuff of the heart" as being the understanding and compassionate beings we were designed to be as our lives unfold into this world?

Gratitude helps us touch all of this and more, and, let's face it, we'd all benefit from *embodying* a little more gratitude in our lives.

So, let's create our own
little gratitude workshop:

When we personally take the time to survey our life and to open our minds in order to see where we're stuck and where we need to heal, it allows us to catch a glimpse of our path to that healing.

I call gratitude the universal healer. When we embrace it, its natural strength can assist us in so many of our personal struggles. Inviting gratitude into any difficult situation immediately helps us take the energetic charge that an issue creates down a notch, and it helps us move toward peace around it. This is because gratitude is ultimately a form of love, and it helps us embrace our life in a gentler and deeper way. And because it is derived through love, it's a gift that reflects who we are, and we're born with the natural ability to embody gratitude and hold it throughout our life.

Gratitude plays a huge part in healing our pain. When we allow it to move through us, it's like putting a soothing salve on a burnt mind and injured heart. It eases the pain, makes our injuries more bearable, and opens us up to seeing life in a way that we were not seeing before its appearance. Explore how it might be possible to approach the problems of your life from new directions, open to those challenges with a quality of gratitude that allows you to move towards healing.

The inspiring thing about gratitude is all that it offers us when we practice it. Through gratitude, we automatically connect to self-love and self-forgiveness, we can participate in an energy where self-respect lives, and lighten our load around any problem. There's no situation where gratitude doesn't help us touch our heart. It truly has a way of calming the savage beast of the mind, helping us see life from a direction that embodies love. It's actually the most user-friendly heart app we have! It's the pixie dust of wellbeing. Take any situation, sprinkle it with gratitude for being, and whatever that situation was, it settles a bit, it becomes gentler. Gratitude, for one, can help heal the broken heart from another. In a very real way, it places you in the freshness of gratitude for what's in front of you right now. The gratitude for a child, spouse, friend, or any blessing helps us balance out and heal our sense of loss in this world.

As you participate in your own very special gratitude workshop, pay attention to yourself, and see who you become, watch what blossoms in your life, and how life unfolds through you in new ways. Gratitude is always an experience worth working towards, and paying attention to.

LFB GRATITUDE EXERCISE

The definition of gratitude is quite simple: the quality of being thankful, being in a state of appreciation.

THE LFB GRATITUDE APPLICATION

- What is gratitude and how does it *look* like when we embrace it?
- How does it *feel* when we merge into life with gratitude being a core part of our nature?
- Who do we *become* when gratitude freely moves through us?

LOOK

Take some meditative time and explore what deep meaning gratitude has for you, when you whisper the word gratitude, how is it held within you. What does gratitude **look** like when we try to define it in our lives? What makes it so powerful for us? How does it **look** when we try to incorporate it into our world? How can we best open to it and invite gratitude into our life? What does our world **look** like, ideally, when we live with more gratitude?

It's not always that easy to dissect a word like gratitude, because gratitude is one of those concepts of the heart that's difficult to put words to; it's more clearly held in the ineffability of a feeling. Our sense of appreciation closely resembles gratitude, and yet gratitude is more than that. It almost needs to be approached from a usage standpoint, defined by a giving of examples of its presence. For example, gratitude is in the room when we talk about understanding the deep appreciation that we feel for life and the wonder of being alive, despite all our difficulties. Or for grandparents, like me, the awareness of gratitude that moves through me when I watch my grandchildren play is beyond profound. And we can feel the same thing with our friends, family, spouses and partners, and in a very real way, even with our pets. All of this awareness creates a sense of gratitude that we hold in our heart. Their internal descriptions are clear – this is what gratitude **looks like**, although the depth of those feelings may often lay beyond our words.

We can be grateful for the simple things: having food, shelter, water to drink, air to breathe. Gratitude often incorporates an acceptance and appreciation for what is. It brings our awareness to right-here, right-now, connected to this moment in front of us. It's a true exercise in being in the New-Now. And gratitude is based in an understanding that this world and our experience in it is a gift; the privilege that we can experience gratitude for our life experience, despite whether or not we like our circumstances. It's as though experiencing gratitude requires us to see the good in our lives, it pushes us to identify and pay healthy attention to all the beauty of life, all the graces that exist around us. We may not always find that graceful strength to walk in gratitude; the capacity to stop and, and in a moment, take a breath and recalibrate ourselves toward some small part of life where gratitude always exists… but when we do touch it, even lightly, life always seems somehow better.

FEEL

And after we've explored how it might **look** to invite gratitude into our lives, to experience this gift of gratitude, despite our tendency or temptation to ignore it, we have to ask ourselves how it **feels**. What does it feel like to embrace and successfully engage this gift of gratitude in our life? Keep in mind it's a feeling, and it may not come with a fountain of words, but gratitude always deeply touches our heart, and the feelings behind it are some of the most profound expressions and experiences that we can come across in our human experience. So, we owe it to ourselves to explore. What does gratitude **feel** like? What is it to walk with appreciation, and a true sense of gratitude that expands our heart into the world? To experience the joy that can be that pivotal point in our journey that shows us that at any moment we can see our lives through the eyes of being grateful. That we can know the graces of gratitude, and that it can come forward, move through us, and help heal us. Gratitude can cultivate the feelings of living a life of pure joy – a joy that can exist despite any circumstance. And that feeling, that gratitude leading us to our joy, is worth feeling, and worth our deepest exploration.

BECOME

And then in our **becoming**, when we walk with gratitude and the joy it cultivates, who are we? Who do we **become** when gratitude is present and moving through us? How do we walk and move through this world when gratitude exists in our heart? And how do we treat others, the people we pass by on a daily basis, our family, friends, and our loved ones? Who do we **become** when we allow our heart to be what it's meant to be through gratitude? Who are we when we invite gratitude to become a primary contributor to the way we experience our world?

Personally, I hold gratitude pretty close. I tend to walk around saying *thank you, thank you, thank you* a lot – usually under my breath, and quietly to myself, sometimes out loud to the world, or directed at creation, or towards all the people who have influenced my life. I get it. It might seem a tad overboard, but it's absolutely a reflection of the feelings of gratitude I have for my life. Yeah, it might catch people by surprise, might sound a little weird, and my partner looks at me like I'm a little crazy sometimes, but she understands me. Which, yes, I am also grateful for. Gratitude. I hold it close.

NOTE: In case you noticed the relationship, being in gratitude allows us to hear the whispers of being present to each new moment. Through it, we can awaken to the gift of being alive to the New-Now. They rely on each other. You can't have the full truth of being present to and alive to the mystery of life unfolding, and not understand what it is to know gratitude.

LFB
SELF-LOVE
what would self-love do?

Self-Love is another great opportunity for some self-exploration. Allow yourself to take the time to **look** at some of the many qualities of self-love. Explore the different forms of its expression, especially as your sense of self-love relates to how you respond to any blockages and struggles that exist in your life. Pay attention to your resistance around any of the ideas about self-love, seeing yourself as enough, belonging in this world, worthy, and making a difference to this world. Include any resistance that is present in your inner world and your outer experience. Your resistance is a great indicator that can show you what you need to work on. Pay attention to what it is to give yourself to life, in a strong but gentle way.

Make a list you can refer to. Be an observer of yourself and watch how those struggles unfold for you. Pay attention to the way you tend to interact and communicate with yourself and others, the different approaches you conduct life with, and question if it's self-loving. This kind of attention to one's self naturally inspires a lot of ideas to explore and consider. It shows us the subjects, behaviors, and thinking we might like to change regarding the way we're living. It shows us where we need to look for our healing and points us toward the growth that's most vital for us to know in our hearts.

So, ask yourself the questions and try and keep track of your answers. What does self-love **look** like?

In letting go of the things that you feel you need control over, and allowing the joy to come through accepting what is (the gift that's been brought to you), actually puts you more in touch with the joy you're truly looking for. It's a joy that you never would have received had you simply gotten what you wanted.

Letting go. This is *self-love*.

That is self-love – to take something that has control over you and to release it so that you can feel joy, or even the simplicity of the absence of anxiety.

Self-love is all encompassing. It naturally includes healthy patience, a sense of kindness that maintains integrity for all, and justice – the kind of justice that's fair to all and leaves no one abused. Is there a self-love that helps you cultivate a strong belief that you belong in this world, a respect for yourself and your journey? And do you appreciate and have gratitude for the deep truth of who you are? Do you walk toward yourself with the same forgiveness in your heart that you bring to those you love most? What does that look like?

Who do you *become* as you begin this journey into loving yourself from a place this world may not have taught us, but from a world that already exists in your own heart? Who do you *become* in this place where the heart's essence meets your world of being?

Who are you when you know and live *self-love*?

www.ingramcontent.com/pod-product-compliance
Lightning Source LLC
Chambersburg PA
CBHW022231080526
44577CB00005B/173